Happy Advent!

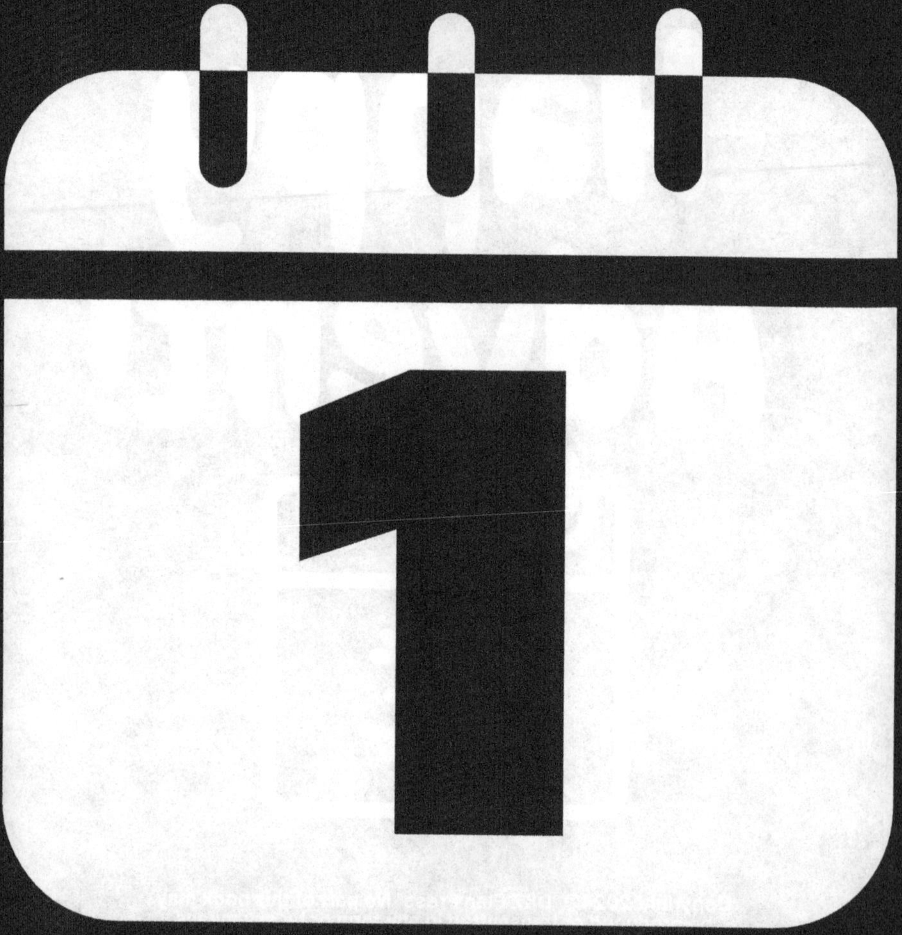
1

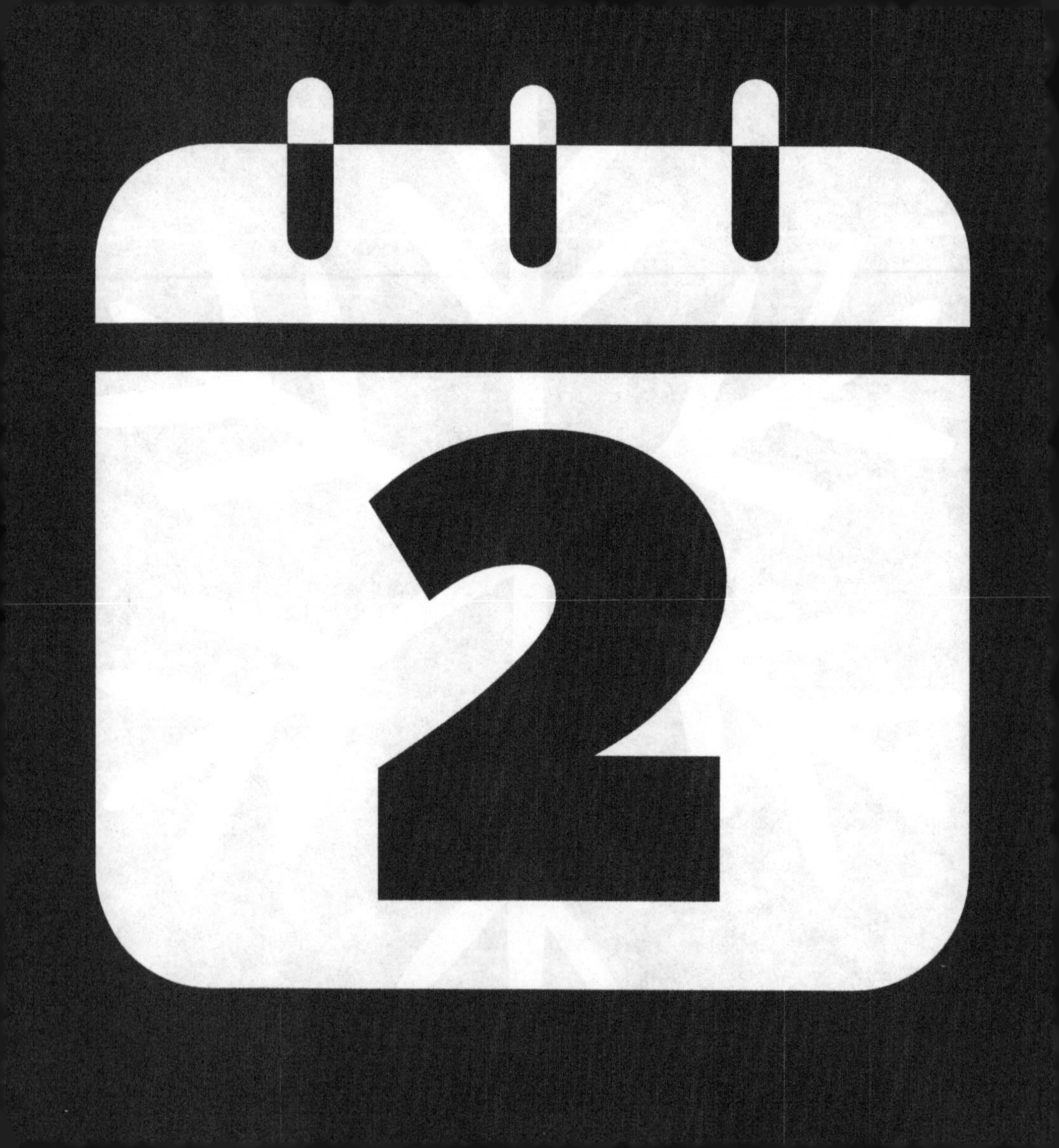
2

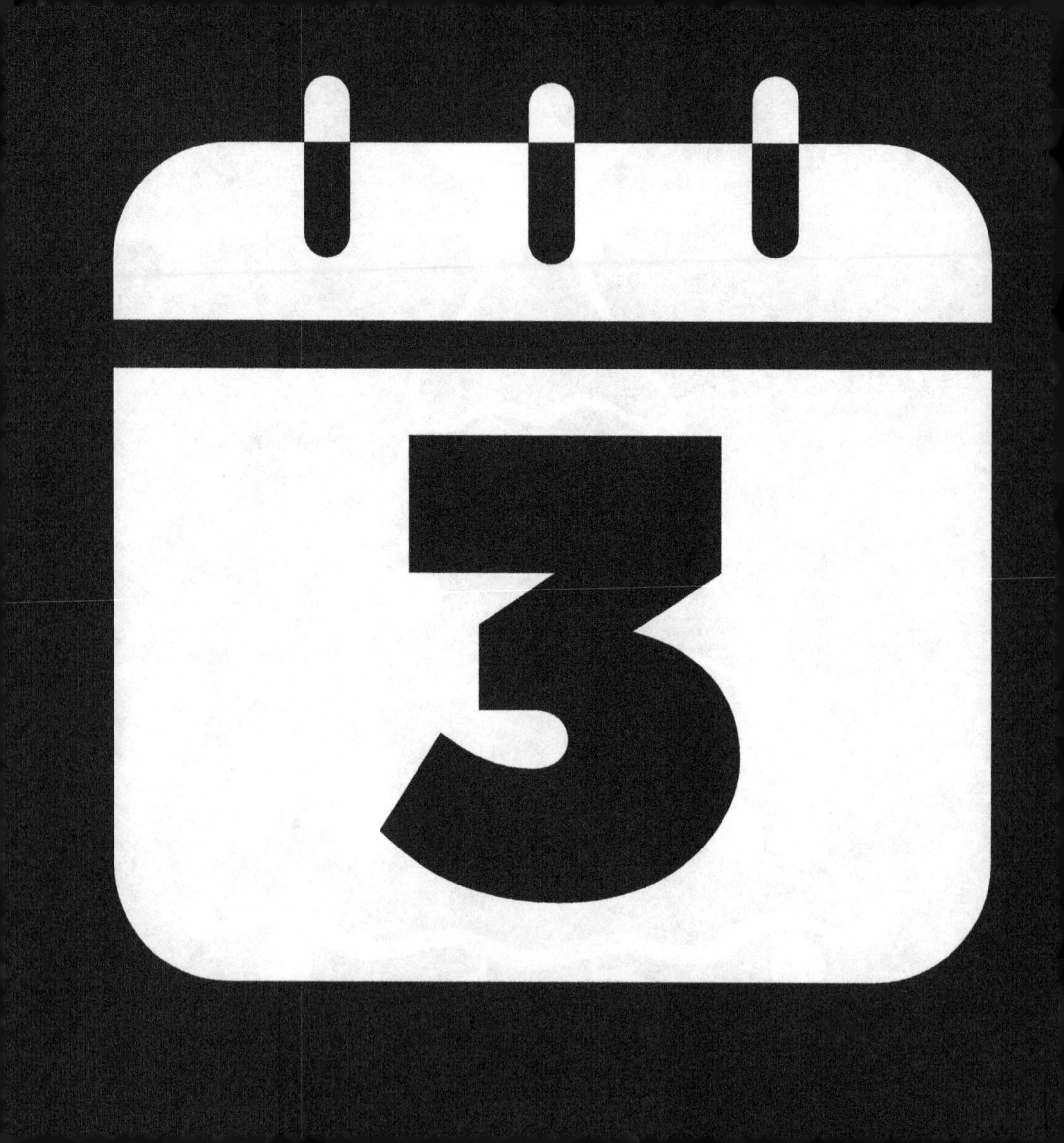
3

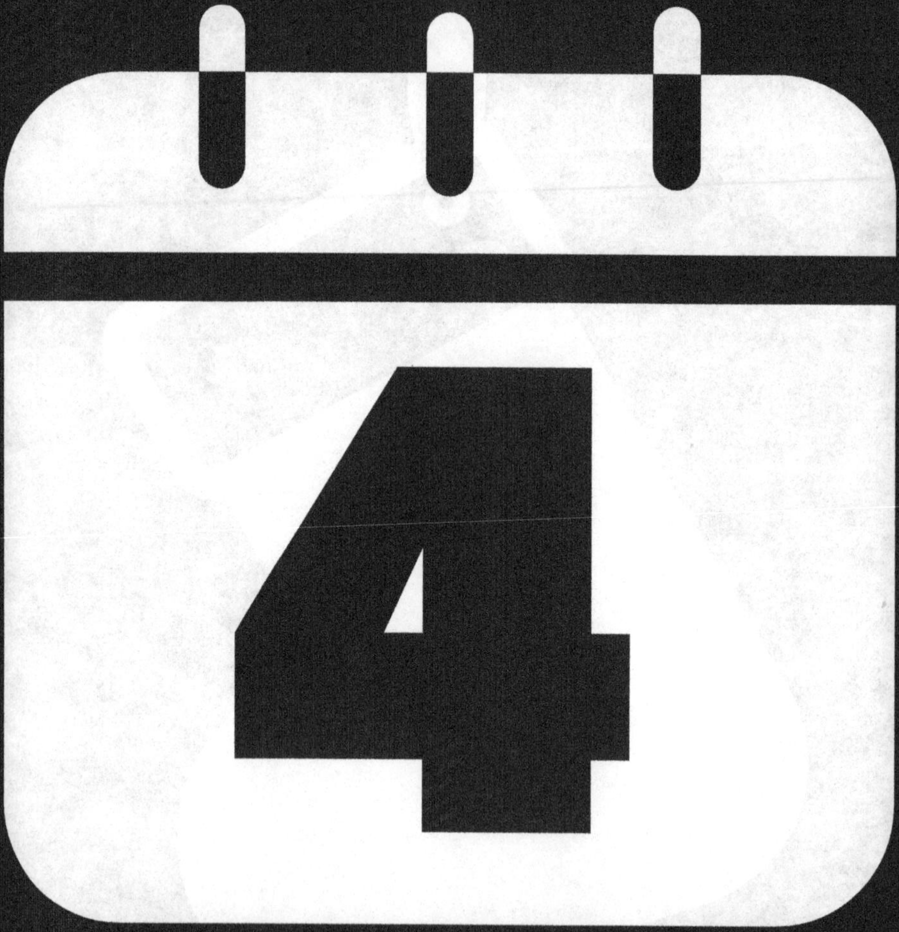
4

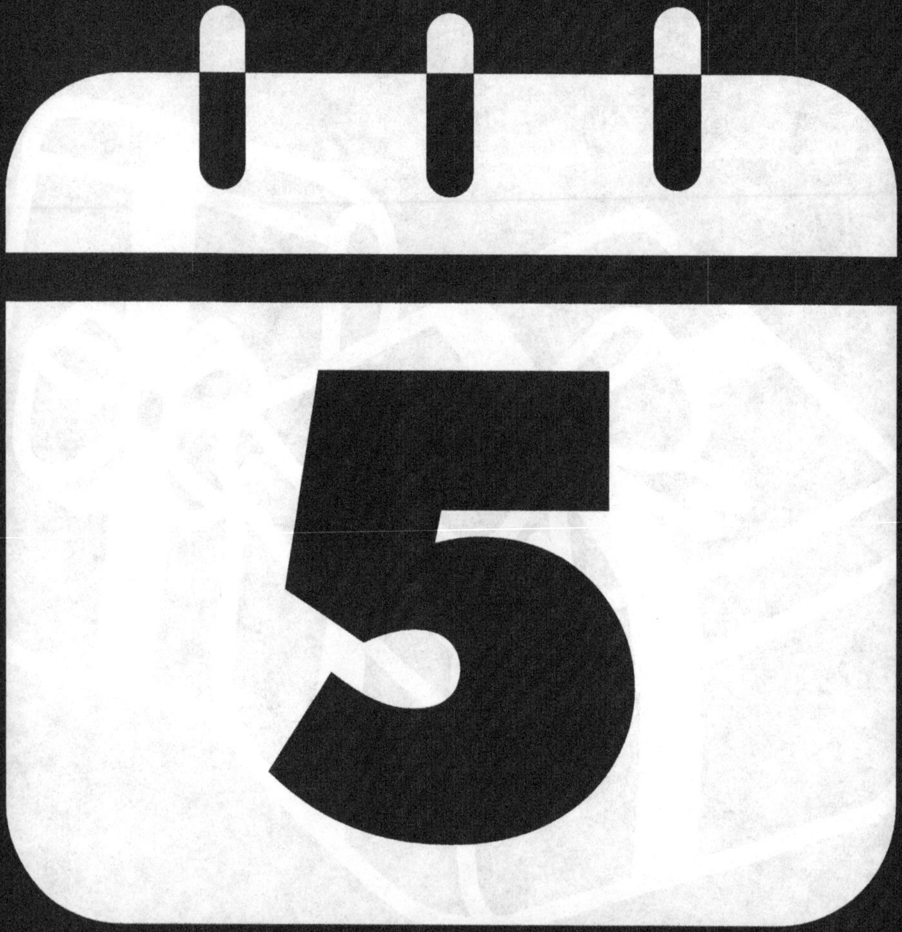
5

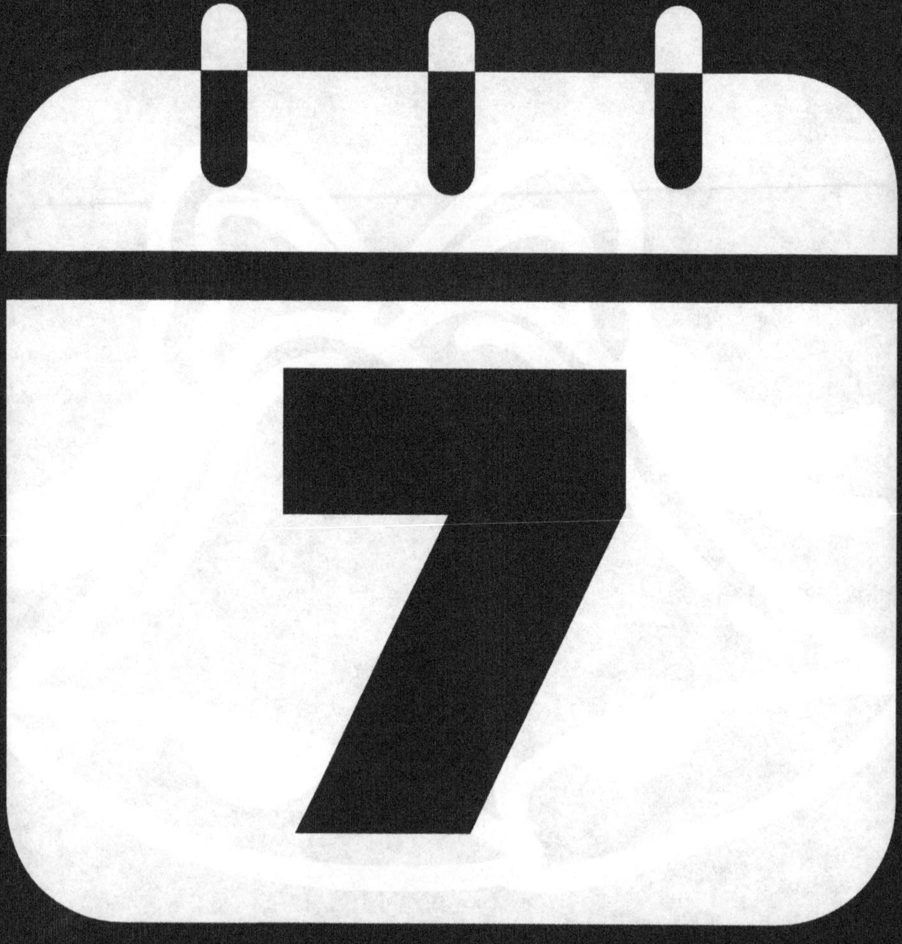
7

8

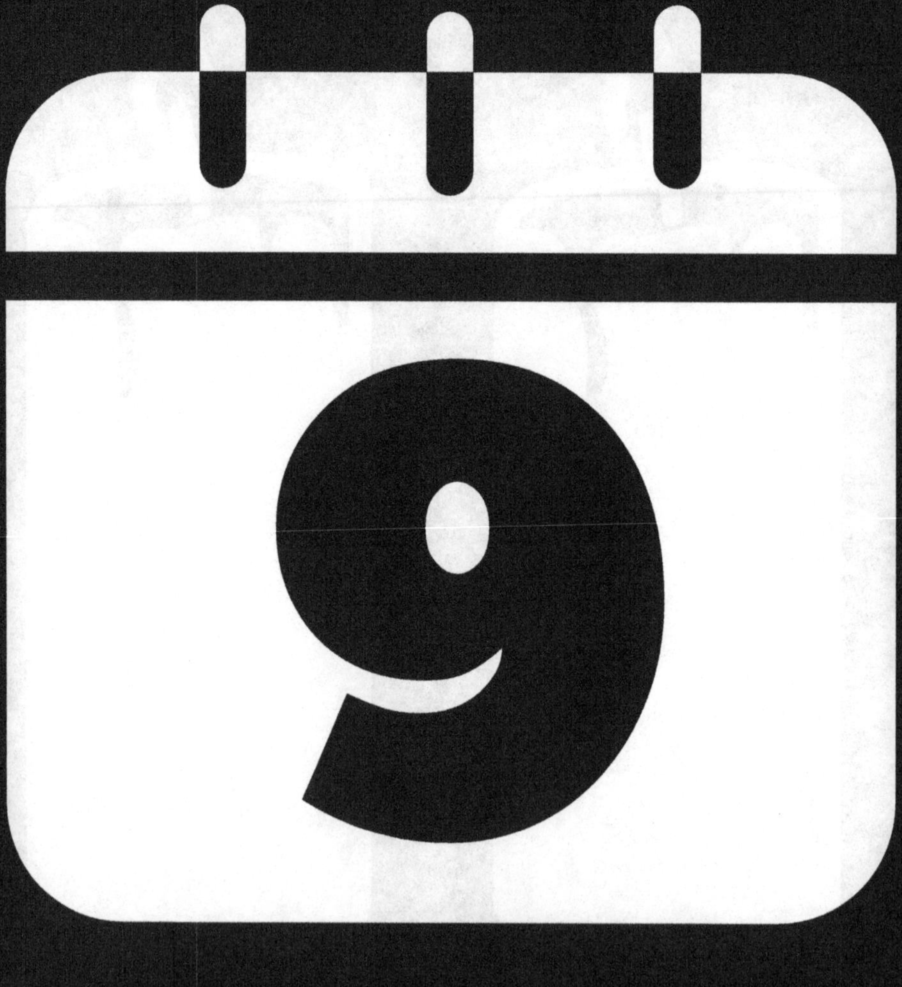
9

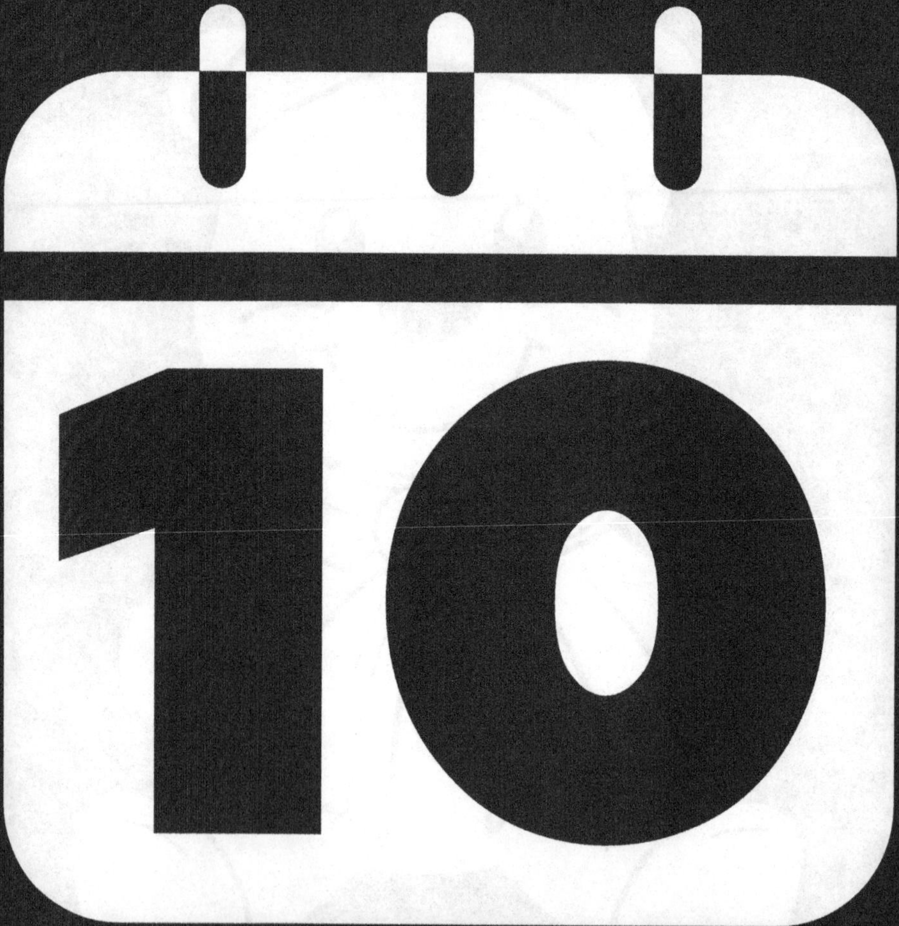
10

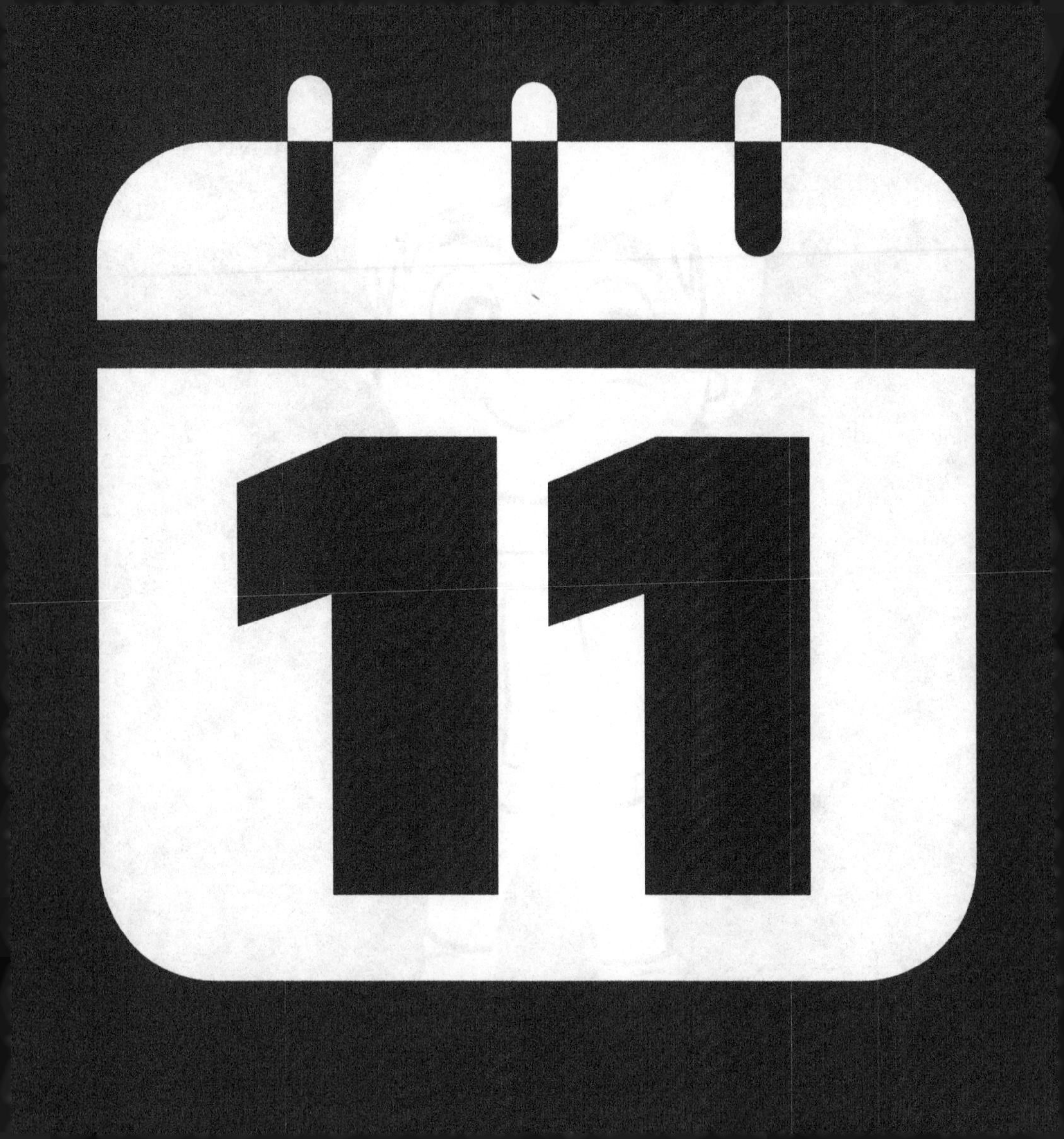
11

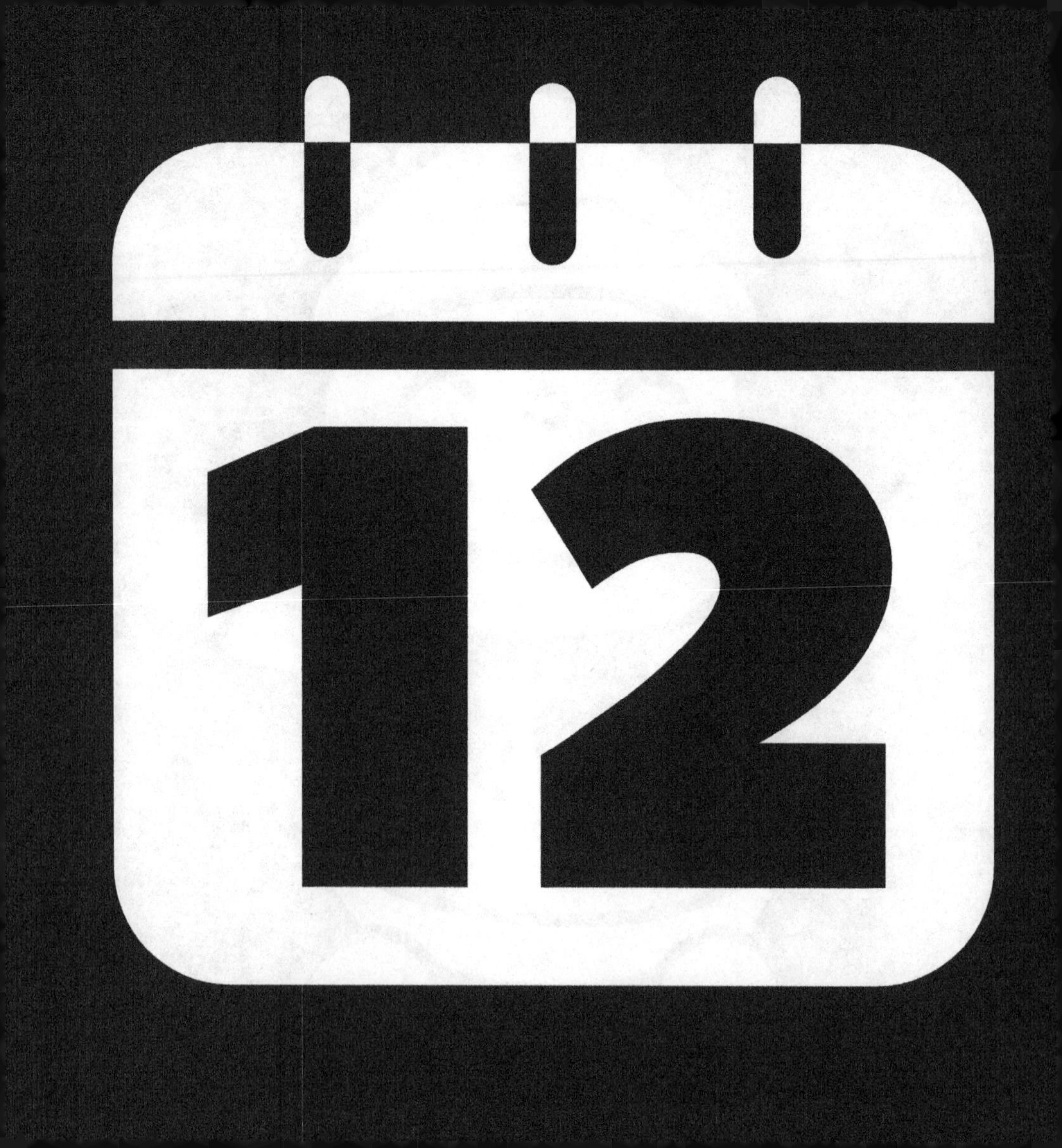
12

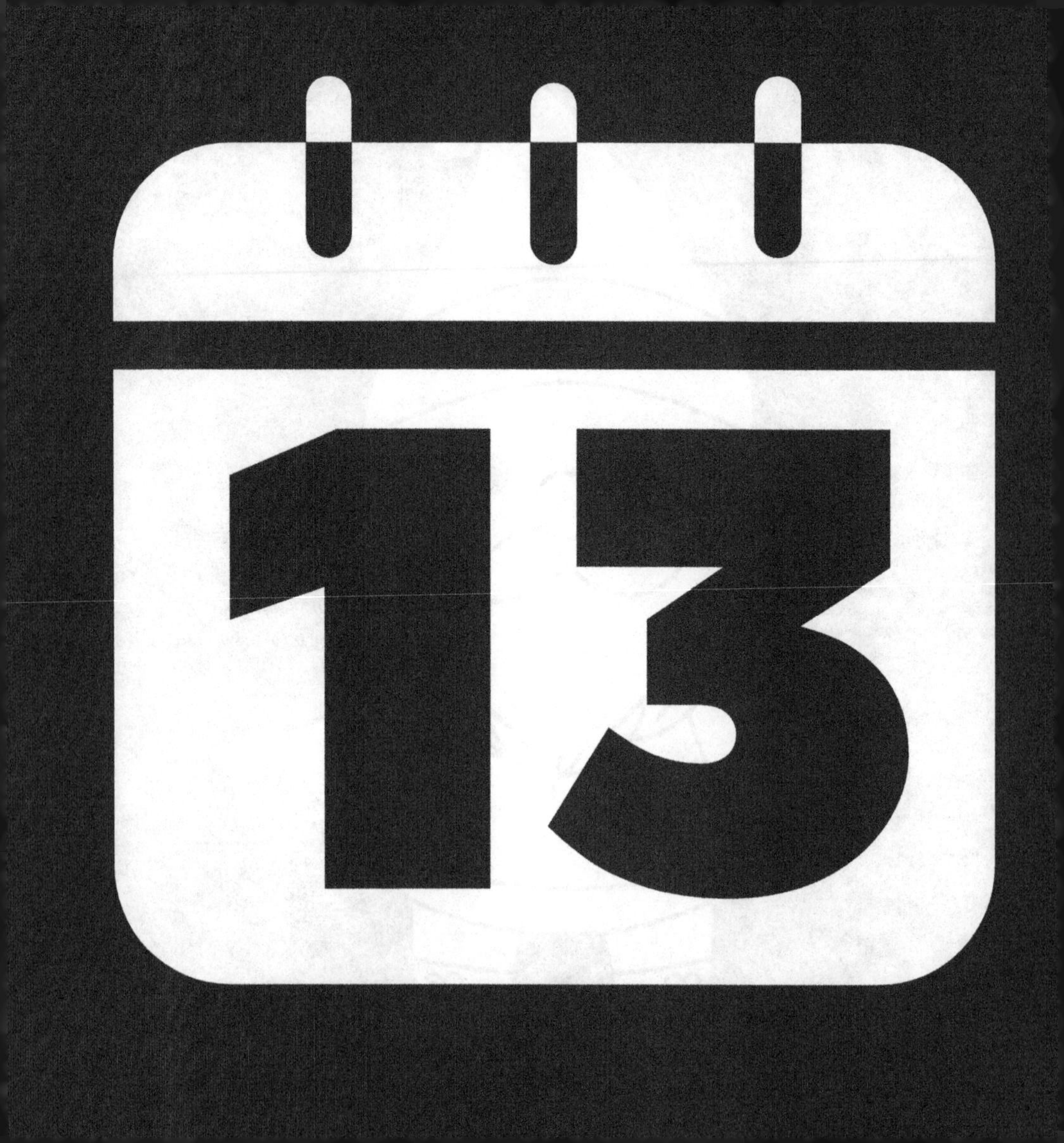
13

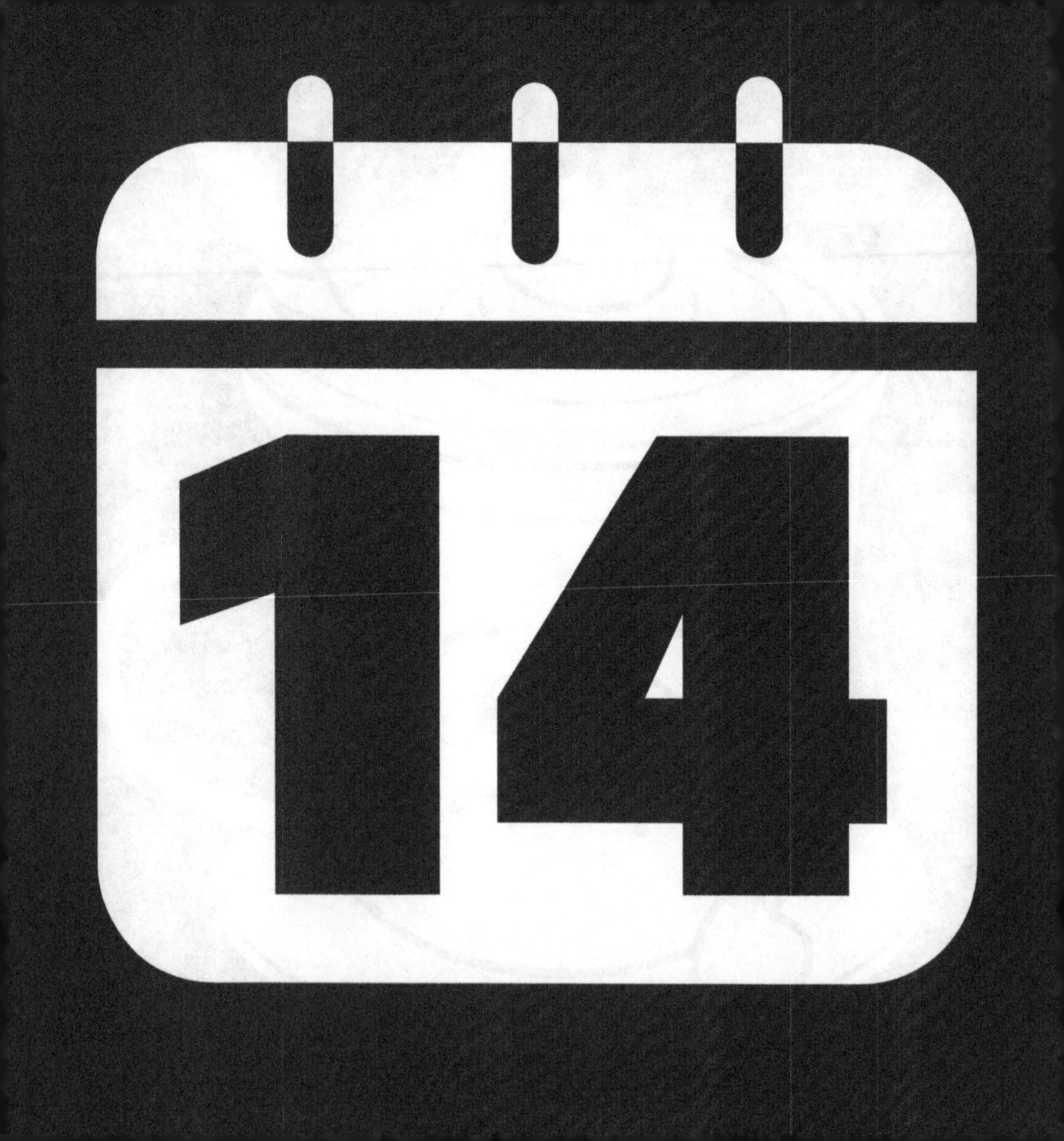
14

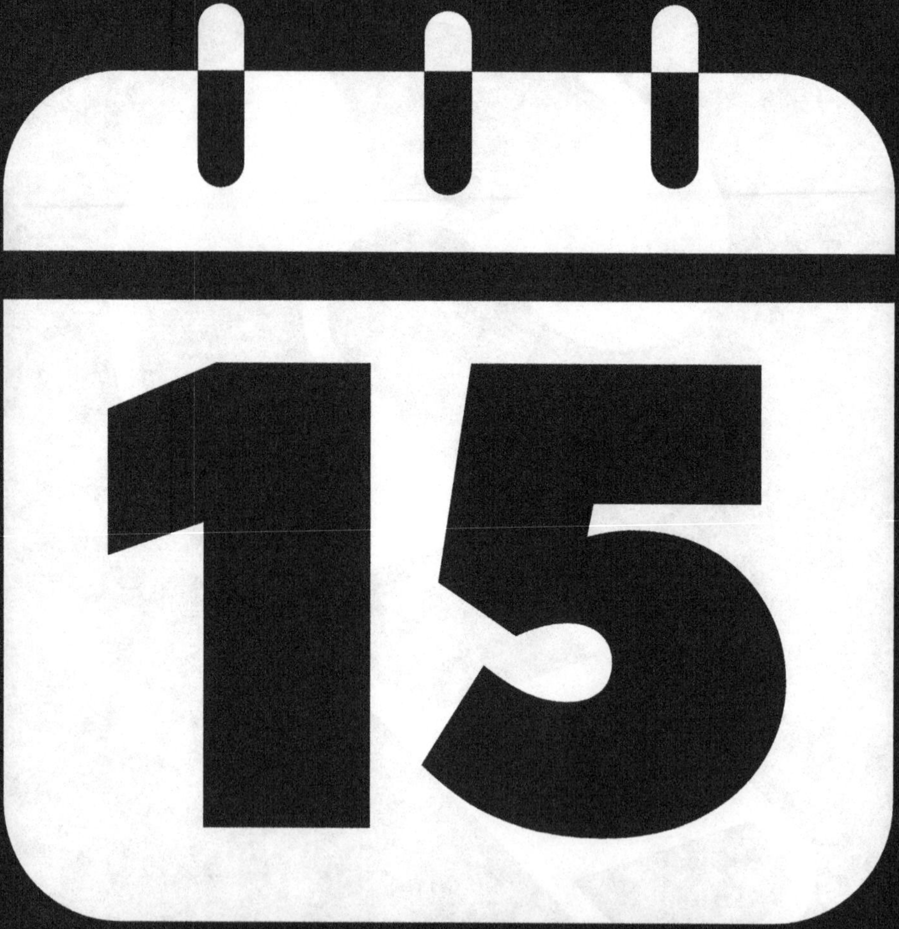
15

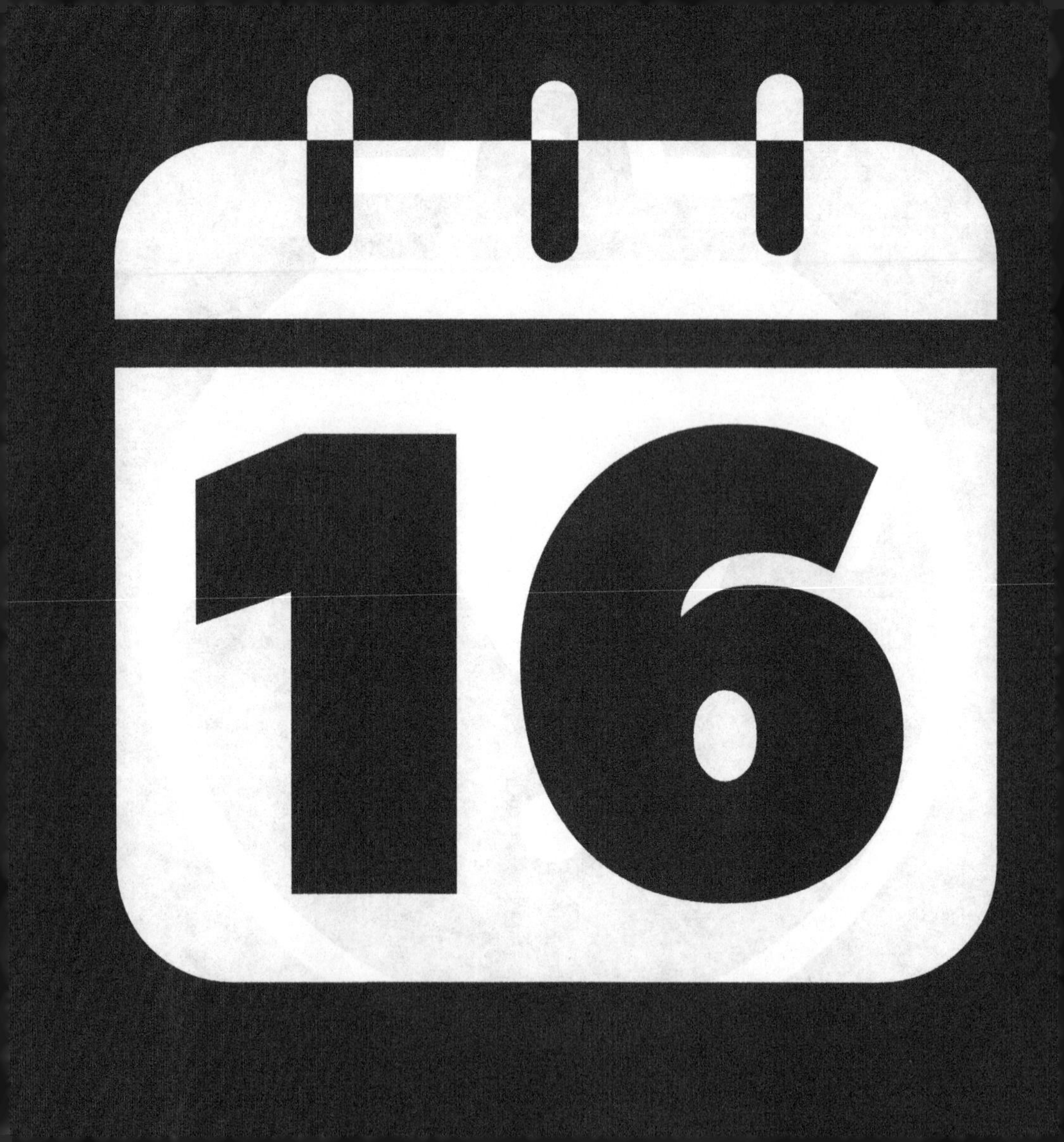
16

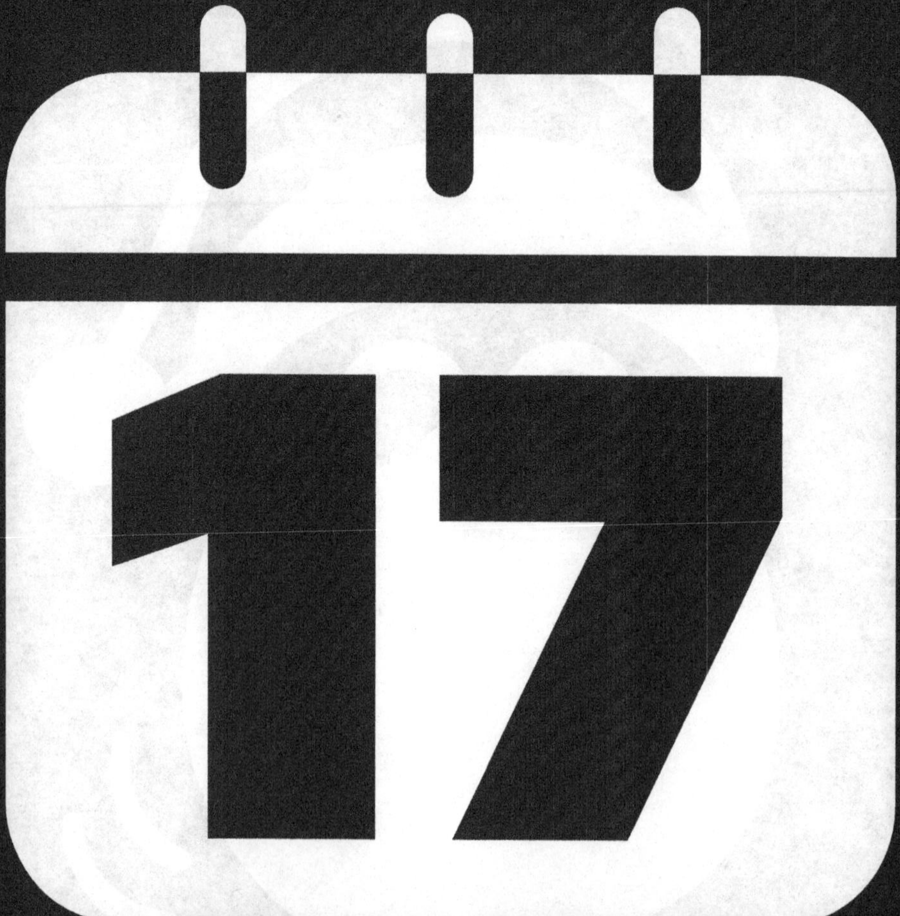
17

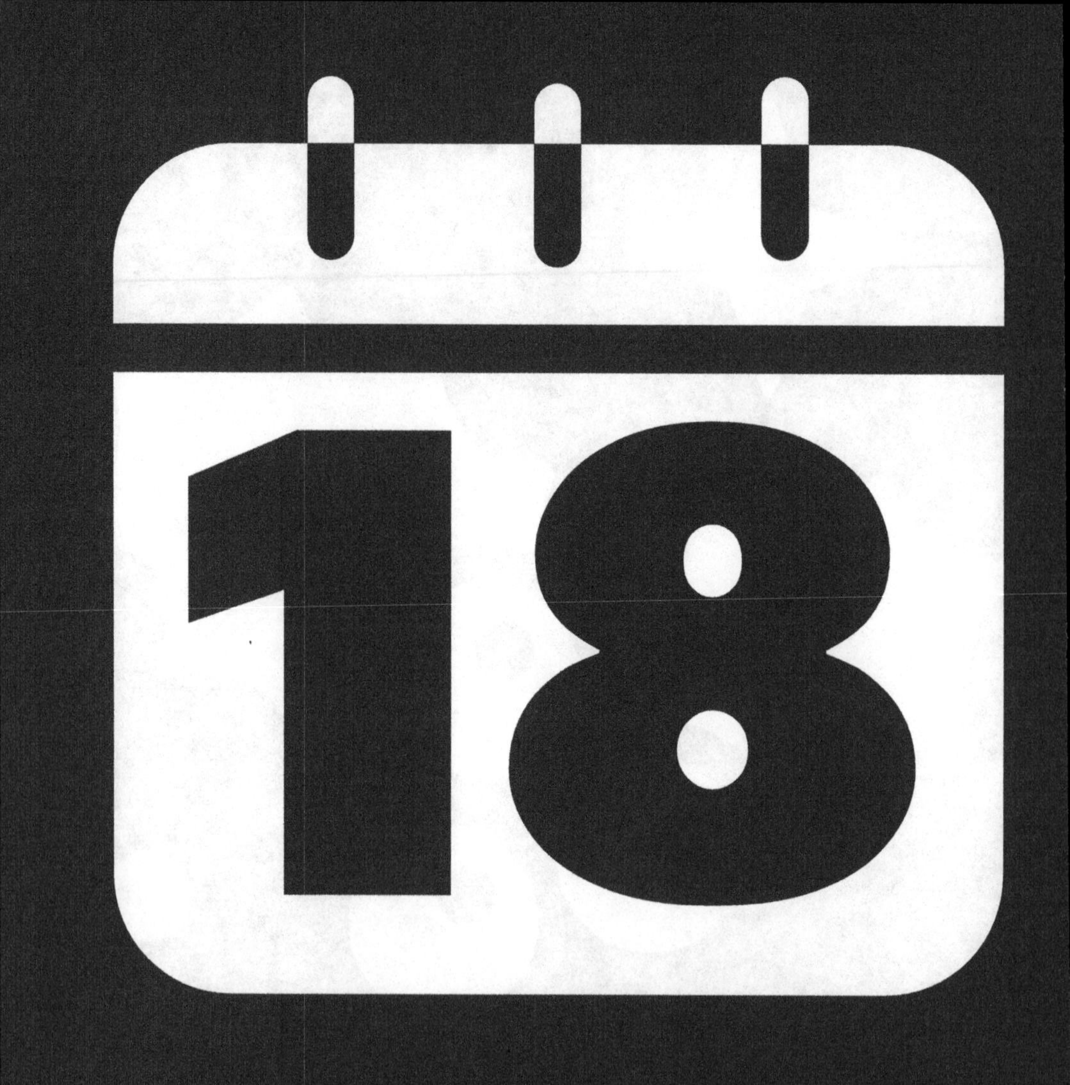
18

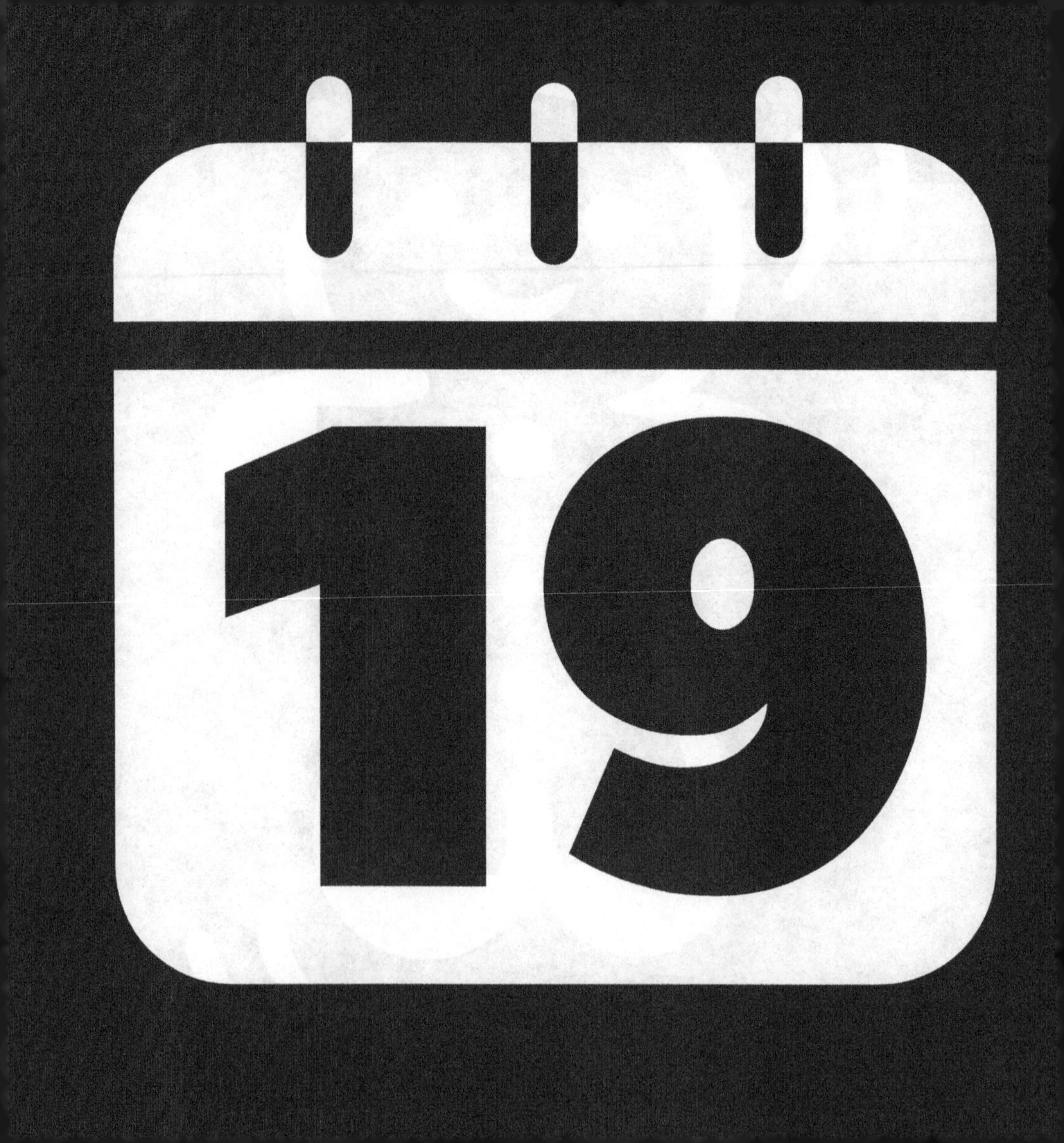
19

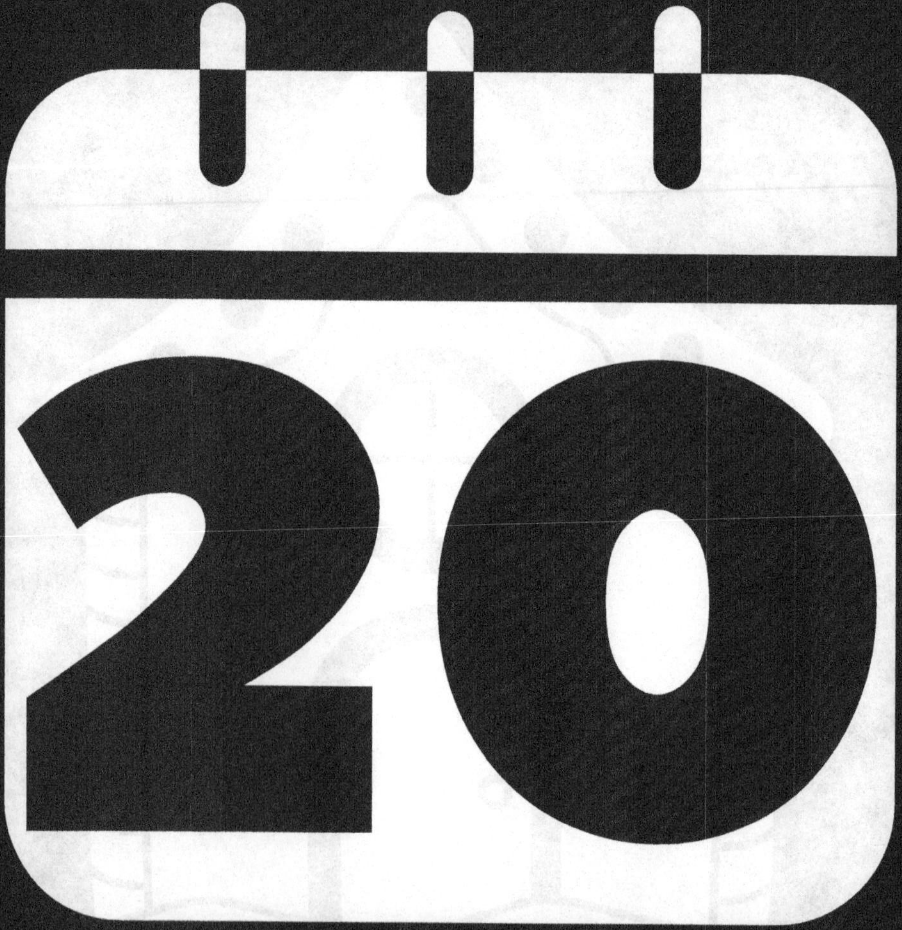
20

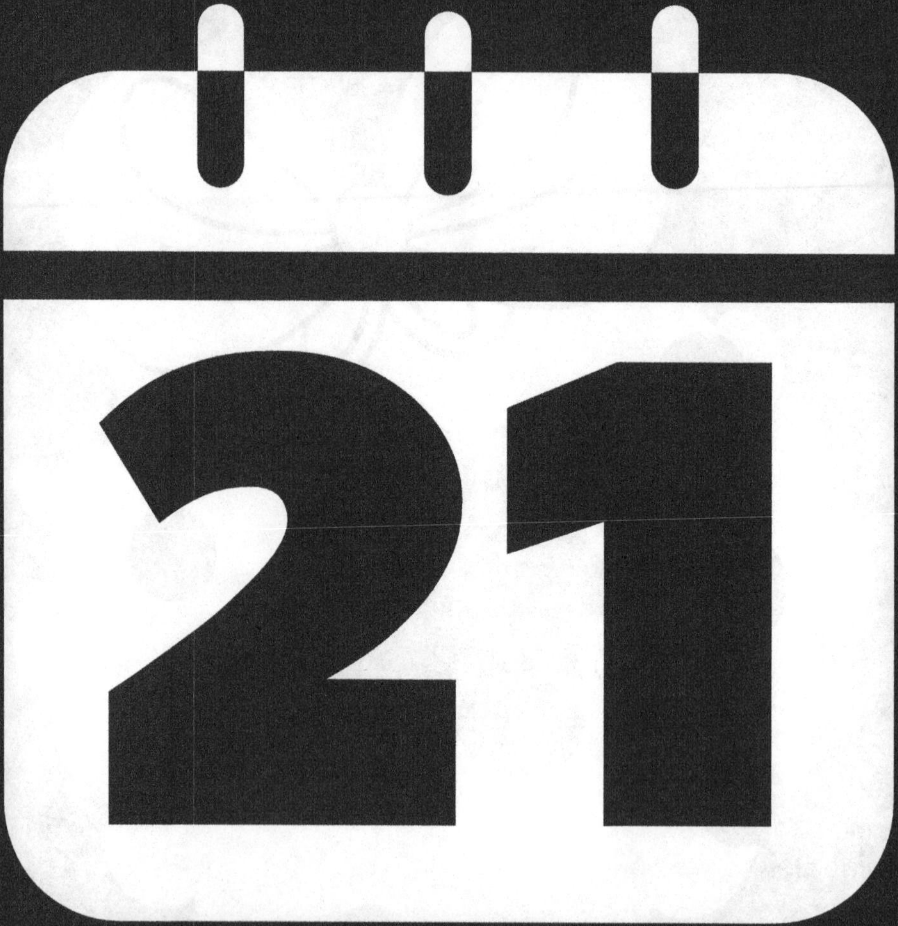
21

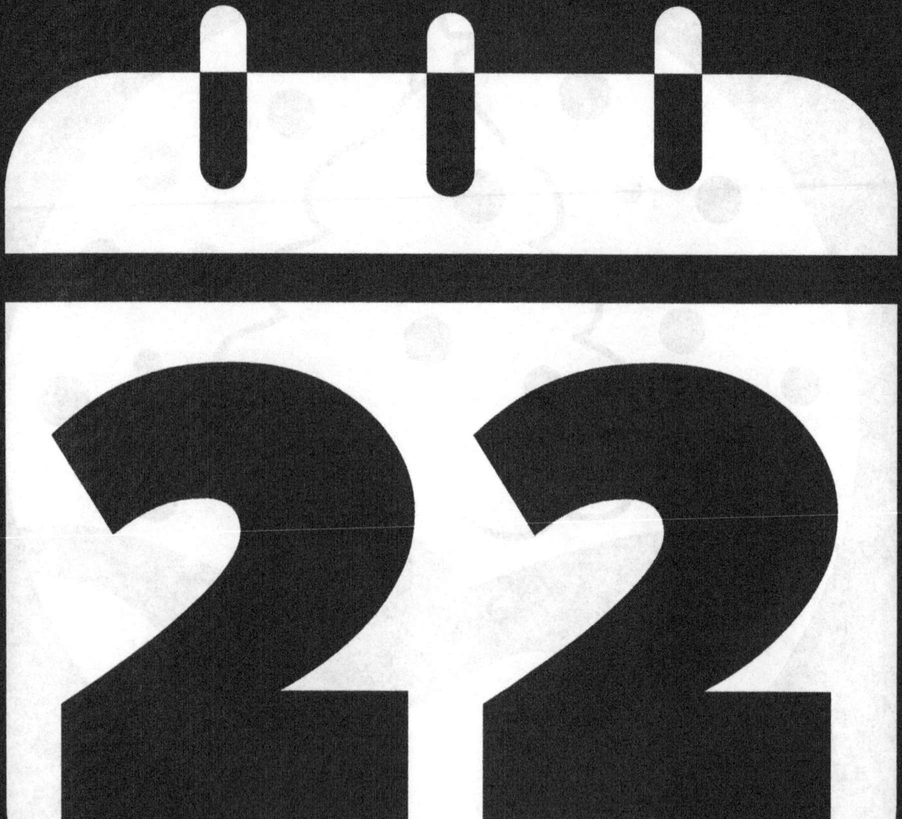
22

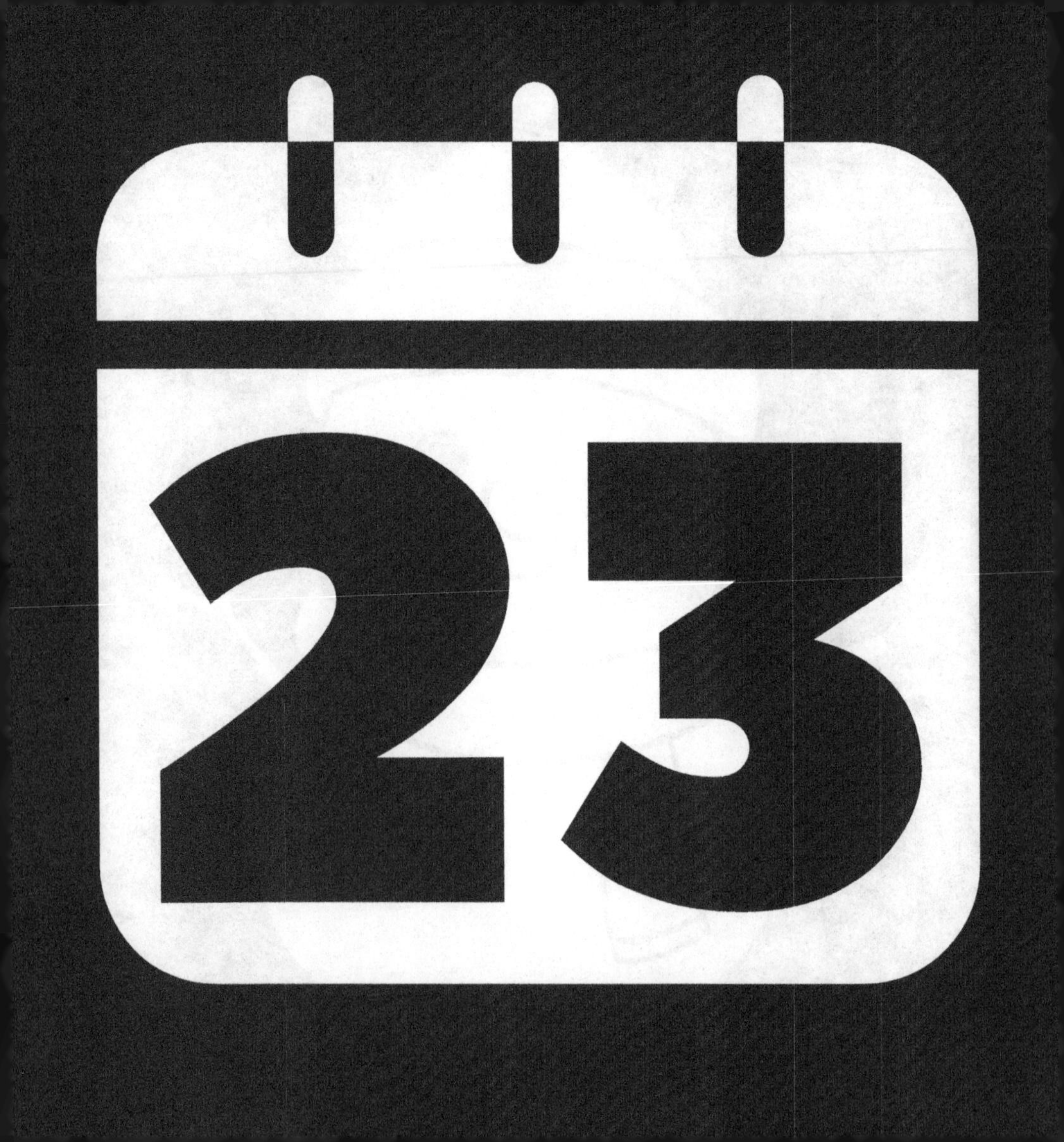
23

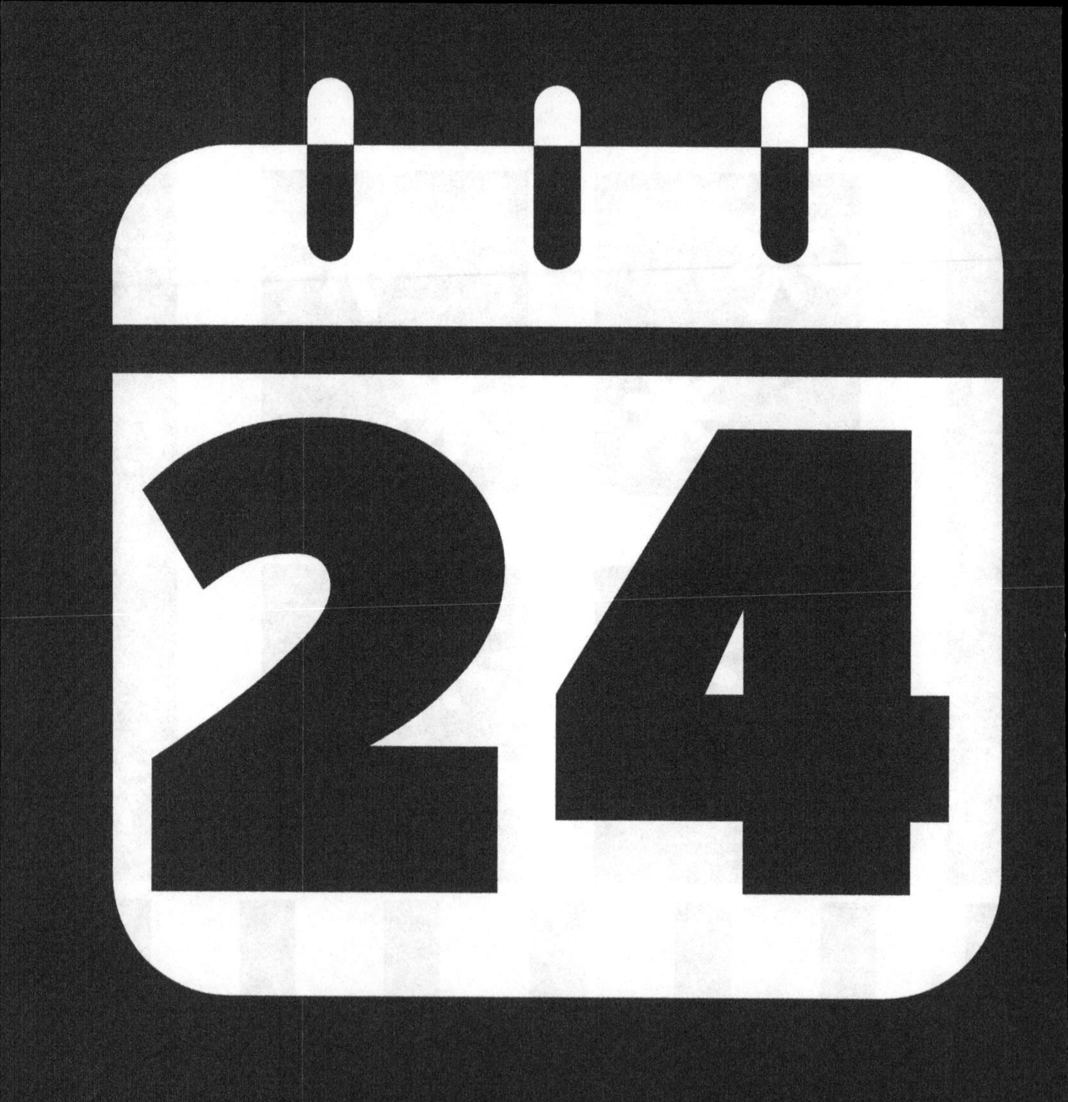
24

IF YOU ENJOYED THIS BOOK, I WOULD GREATLY APPRECIATE IT IF YOU COULD TAKE A MOMENT TO SHARE YOUR THOUGHTS. YOUR FEEDBACK MEANS THE WORLD TO ME, AND YOUR REVIEW WILL HELP OTHERS DISCOVER THIS BOOK AND MAKE THEIR HOLIDAY SEASON SPECIAL.
THANK YOU FOR YOUR SUPPORT, AND I WISH YOU A MERRY CHRISTMAS AND A HAPPY NEW YEAR!

AMAZON AUTHOR PAGES:

@D&Z Plan Press

72131999R00030